Kelly

CW00801445

by Iain Gray

Lang**Syne**

PUBLISHING

WRITING *to* REMEMBER

LangSyne

PUBLISHING

WRITING *to* REMEMBER

Vineyard Business Centre,
Pathhead, Midlothian EH37 5XP
Tel: 01875 321 203 Fax: 01875 321 233
E-mail: info@lang-syne.co.uk
www.langsyneshop.co.uk

Design by Dorothy Meikle
Printed by Montgomery Litho, Glasgow
© Lang Syne Publishers Ltd 2011

ISBN 978-1-85217-261-9

Kelly

MOTTO:
God is my tower of strength.

CREST:
The green enfield.

NAME variations include:
Ó Ceallaigh *(Gaelic)*
Kelley
Kellie
Kilkelly
MacKillely
O'Kelly
Gilkelly
O'Cadhla
MacGoila

Chapter one:
Origins of Irish surnames

According to an old saying, there are two types of Irish – those who actually are Irish and those who wish they were.

This sentiment is only one example of the allure that the high romance and drama of the proud nation's history holds for thousands of people scattered across the world today.

It's a sad fact, however, that the vast majority of Irish surnames are found far beyond Irish shores, rather than on the Emerald Isle itself.

The population stood at around eight million souls in 1841, but today it stands at fewer than six million.

This is mainly a tragic consequence of the potato famine, also known as the Great Hunger, which devastated Ireland between 1845 and 1849.

The Irish peasantry had become almost wholly reliant for basic sustenance on the potato, first introduced from the Americas in the seventeenth century.

When the crop was hit by a blight, at least 800,000 people starved to death while an estimated two million others were forced to seek a new life far from their native shores – particularly in America, Canada, and Australia.

The effects of the potato blight continued until about 1851, by which time a firm pattern of emigration had become established.

Ireland's loss, however, was to the gain of the countries in which the immigrants settled, contributing enormously, as their descendants do today, to the well being of the nations in which their forefathers settled.

But those who were forced through dire circumstance to establish a new life in foreign parts never forgot their roots, or the proud heritage and traditions of the land that gave them birth.

Nor do their descendants.

It is a heritage that is inextricably bound up in the colourful variety of Irish names themselves – and the origin and history of these names forms an integral part of the vibrant drama that is the nation's history, one of both glorious fortune and tragic misfortune.

This history is well documented, and one of the most important and fascinating of the earliest sources are *The Annals of the Four Masters*, compiled between 1632 and 1636 by four friars at the Franciscan Monastery in County Donegal.

Compiled from earlier sources, and purporting to go back to the Biblical Deluge, much of the material takes in the mythological origins and history of Ireland and the Irish.

This includes tales of successive waves of invaders and settlers such as the Fomorians, the Partholonians, the Nemedians, the Fir Bolgs, the Tuatha De Danann, and the Laigain.

Of particular interest are the *Milesian Genealogies*,

because the majority of Irish clans today claim a descent from either Heremon, Ir, or Heber – three of the sons of Milesius, a king of what is now modern day Spain.

These sons invaded Ireland in the second millennium B.C, apparently in fulfilment of a mysterious prophecy received by their father.

This Milesian lineage is said to have ruled Ireland for nearly 3,000 years, until the island came under the sway of England's King Henry II in 1171 following what is known as the Cambro-Norman invasion.

This is an important date not only in Irish history in general, but for the effect the invasion subsequently had for Irish surnames.

'Cambro' comes from the Welsh, and 'Cambro-Norman' describes those Welsh knights of Norman origin who invaded Ireland.

But they were invaders who stayed, inter-marrying with the native Irish population and founding their own proud dynasties that bore Cambro-Norman names such as Archer, Barbour, Brannagh, Fitzgerald, Fitzgibbon, Fleming, Joyce, Plunkett, and Walsh – to name only a few.

These 'Cambro-Norman' surnames that still flourish throughout the world today form one of the three main categories in which Irish names can be placed – those of Gaelic-Irish, Cambro-Norman, and Anglo-Irish.

Previous to the Cambro-Norman invasion of the twelfth century, and throughout the earlier invasions and settlement of those wild bands of sea rovers known as the Vikings in the eighth and ninth centuries, the population of the island was relatively small, and it was normal for a person to be identified through the use of only a forename.

But as population gradually increased and there were many more people with the same forename, surnames were adopted to distinguish one person, or one community, from another.

Individuals identified themselves with their own particular tribe, or 'tuath', and this tribe – that also became known as a clann, or clan – took its name from some distinguished ancestor who had founded the clan.

The Gaelic-Irish form of the name Kelly, for example, is Ó Ceallaigh, or O'Kelly, indicating descent from an original 'Ceallaigh', with the 'O' denoting 'grandson of.' The name was later anglicised to Kelly.

The prefix 'Mac' or 'Mc', meanwhile, as with the clans of the Scottish Highlands, denotes 'son of.'

Although the Irish clans had much in common with their Scottish counterparts, one important difference lies in what are known as 'septs', or branches, of the clan.

Septs of Scottish clans were groups who often bore an entirely different name from the clan name but were under the clan's protection.

In Ireland, septs were groups that shared the same name and who could be found scattered throughout the four provinces of Ulster, Leinster, Munster, and Connacht.

The 'golden age' of the Gaelic-Irish clans, infused as their veins were with the blood of Celts, pre-dates the Viking invasions of the eighth and ninth centuries and the Norman invasion of the twelfth century, and the sacred heart of the country was the Hill of Tara, near the River Boyne, in County Meath.

Known in Gaelic as 'Teamhar na Rí', or Hill of Kings, it was the royal seat of the 'Ard Rí Éireann', or High King of Ireland, to whom the petty kings, or chieftains, from the island's provinces were ultimately subordinate.

It was on the Hill of Tara, beside a stone pillar known as the Irish 'Lia Fáil', or Stone of Destiny, that the High Kings were inaugurated and, according to legend, this stone would emit a piercing screech that could be heard all over Ireland when touched by the hand of the rightful king.

The Hill of Tara is today one of the island's main tourist attractions.

Opposition to English rule over Ireland, established in the wake of the Cambro-Norman invasion, broke out frequently and the harsh solution adopted by the powerful forces of the Crown was to forcibly evict the native Irish from their lands.

These lands were then granted to Protestant colonists, or 'planters', from Britain.

Many of these colonists, ironically, came from Scotland and were the descendants of the original 'Scotti', or 'Scots', who gave their name to Scotland after migrating there in the fifth century A.D., from the north of Ireland.

Colonisation entailed harsh penal laws being imposed on the majority of the native Irish population, stripping them practically of all of their rights.

The Crown's main bastion in Ireland was Dublin and its environs, known as the Pale, and it was the dispossessed peasantry who lived outside this Pale, desperately striving to eke out a meagre living.

It was this that gave rise to the modern-day expression of someone or something being 'beyond the pale'.

Attempts were made to stamp out all aspects of the ancient Gaelic-Irish culture, to the extent that even to bear a Gaelic-Irish name was to invite discrimination.

This is why many Gaelic-Irish names were anglicised with, for example, and noted above, Ó Ceallaigh, or O'Kelly, being anglicised to Kelly.

Succeeding centuries have seen strong revivals of Gaelic-Irish consciousness, however, and this has led to many families reverting back to the original form of their name, while the language itself is frequently found on the fluent tongues of an estimated 90,000 to 145,000 of the island's population.

Ireland's turbulent history of religious and political strife is one that lasted well into the twentieth century, a landmark century that saw the partition of the island into the twenty-six counties of the independent Republic of

Ireland, or Eire, and the six counties of Northern Ireland, or Ulster.

Dublin, originally founded by Vikings, is now a vibrant and truly cosmopolitan city while the proud city of Belfast is one of the jewels in the crown of Ulster.

It was Saint Patrick who first brought the light of Christianity to Ireland in the fifth century A.D.

Interpretations of this Christian message have varied over the centuries, often leading to bitter sectarian conflict – but the many intricately sculpted Celtic Crosses found all over the island are symbolic of a unity that crosses the sectarian divide.

It is an image that fuses the 'old gods' of the Celts with Christianity.

All the signs from the early years of this new millennium indicate that sectarian strife may soon become a thing of the past – with the Irish and their many kinsfolk across the world, be they Protestant or Catholic, finding common purpose in the rich tapestry of their shared heritage.

Chapter two:

A royal tribe

The Irish are justly renowned for their hospitality, and anyone who receives a great welcome is said to have been the recipient of 'the welcome of the O'Kellys.'

The roots of the expression can be traced back to more than six hundred years ago, to 1351, when William Boy O'Kelly hosted what is reputed to have been the biggest feast in Irish history at his castle on the shores of beautiful Lough Ree.

Among his many guests at the month-long jamboree were some of the island's greatest musicians, poets, and story tellers, and it was William Boy O'Kelly's love of learning and the ancient traditions of his proud family name that led to him laying the groundwork for what became nearly fifty years later *The Book of O'Kellys*.

Compiled from a number of earlier sources, written by six scribes, and now in the care of the Royal Irish Academy, *The Book of O'Kellys* provides a fascinating insight into the origins and genealogies of the Kellys.

' Kelly' is the anglicised version of the Irish-Gaelic Ó Ceallaigh, or O'Kelly, and related names include Kelley, Kellie, Kilkelly, MacKillely, Gilkelly, O'Cadhla, and MacGoila.

'Ceallaigh', 'Ceallach', or 'Callach', is reputed to have

been an early tenth century Irish warrior, and the name itself is said to signify 'strife', 'war', or 'contention', although one source also gives 'bright-headed.'

Not all Kellys, in all the rich variety of spellings of the name, can be traced back to the same source, and septs of the name flourished for centuries throughout the length and breadth of the island.

These main septs were the O'Kellys of Ú Máine, the O'Kellys of Breagh, the O'Kellys of Ulster, the O'Kellys of Cork, the O'Kellys of Sligo, the O'Kellys of Co. Down, the O'Kellys of Laois, and the O'Kellys of Wexford.

By far the most powerful were the O'Kellys of Úi Máine, who traced a descent back to the mighty warrior chief Maine Mor.

'Úi Máine' (also known as Hy Many) means 'Maine's territory', and this was a vast territory that comprised the bulk of the province of Connacht in addition to large areas of what are the modern-day counties of Roscommon and Galway.

Maine Mor and his kinsfolk are believed to have originally hailed from the north of Ireland, and when they arrived in what would become their new homeland in about 457 A.D. it was the territory of the mysterious tribe known as the Fir Bolg.

Thought to have migrated to Ireland from foreign shores at the very dawn of history, they were also known as the Euerni, or Erainn, a name that gradually evolved over the centuries to become the name of the island itself – Eire, or Ireland.

The leader of the Fir Bolg at the time of Maine Mor's arrival was Cian, who agreed to allow him and his kinsfolk to settle, but only after important hostages had been exchanged.

These hostages included one of Maine Mor's sons, who was lodged in the home of the Fir Bolg's brehon, or lawmaker.

After the brehon's wife fell in love with the dashing young son of Maine Mor, the furious brehon managed to persuade Cian to have him killed.

Realising his rash action could have dire consequences for his people, a contrite Cian invited Maine Mor and his warriors to a grand feast – where matters appear to have been resolved to the satisfaction of both sides.

It was this Maine Mor who was the ancestor of Ceallach, from whom the Kelly name derives.

Some Kellys, however, trace a descent from the fourth century King Colla da Crioch, while the O'Kellys of Ulster trace a descent back to Eoghan, a son of the fabled Niall of the Nine Hostages.

The O'Kellys of Cork are said to derive their name from 'na coille', meaning 'from the forests.'

The O'Kellys of Breagh, of present day Co. Meath, had the distinction of being – along with the Connollys,

O'Regans, and O'Harts – among what were known as the Four Royal Tribes of Tara.

This 'dates' the O'Kellys of Breagh back to at least 200 A.D. when Tara was established by the Tuatha De Danann as the inauguration site and seat of the Irish Ard-Rí, or High Kings.

But much of their rich farmlands in the fertile valley of the river Boyne were devastated in the early fourteenth century when Edward Bruce, a brother of the great Scottish warrior king Robert the Bruce, invaded Ireland.

The links between Ireland and Scotland have always been strong, with both nations part of the Celtic 'Gaeltacht', and these ties were no less strong than during Scotland's bloody Wars of Independence with England, when Ireland also suffered under England's imperialist designs.

Normans had invaded Ireland between 1167 and 1169, marking the start of a bitter struggle between the native Irish and the English that would last for centuries.

Rory O'Connor, who died in 1175, was the last native High King of Ireland, and by 1272 the English had conquered Ulster, east of Lough Neagh, in Meath, and most of Munster and Connacht.

Recognising a common enemy in the English, Robert the Bruce sent a remarkable letter to 'all the kings of Ireland, to the prelates and clergy, and to the inhabitants of all Ireland, his friends'.

Appealing to the common traditions and culture of both Scotland and Ireland, Bruce went so far as to refer to both nations being as one.

Edward Bruce sailed from Ayr in May of 1315 (nearly a year after his brother's memorable victory over the English at the battle of Bannockburn) in a fleet of 300 galleys carrying 6,000 veteran soldiers.

Landing on the coast of Antrim on May 26, he quickly rallied fellow Celtic support in his daring bid to defeat the occupying Anglo-Irish forces that owed allegiance to England's Edward II. Bruce gained a series of stunning victories in the initial months of his campaign, including the capture of both Carrickfergus and Dundalk, where all the inhabitants of Dundalk were put to the sword.

The campaign was fought during a grim period in Europe's history when, between 1315 and 1318, a series of crop failures led to the Great European Famine.

The Kellys were among the thousands of native Irish who suffered.

One Irish annalist recorded how '… it was said truly that some evil men were so distraught by famine that they dragged out of cemeteries the corpses of the buried, and roasted the bodies on spits and ate every single one of them; and women ate their sons for hunger.'

Adding to the misery and horror of famine was the vicious warfare sweeping the land in the form of Edward Bruce's army and the forces of the Anglo-Irish.

Bruce is believed to have been inaugurated as High King of Ireland on May 2, 1316.

The Anglo-Irish forces rallied, and the next two years were marked by a bloody series of advances and reversals for Bruce until, in October of 1318, he was killed in a battle fought at Fochart, near Dundalk.

The latter stages of Bruce's campaign had been marked by particularly ferocious warfare throughout the territory of the O'Kellys of Breagh, and they never fully recovered from the devastation caused.

Chapter three:

On the field of battle

**From whichever part of Ireland the Kellys of today
originally hail, what they have in common is that they
are recognised by the Clan Kelly Association as 'Muintir
Ui Cheallaigh', or 'Ceallach's People', and share the
proud motto of 'God is my tower of strength.'**

Their crest, meanwhile, is surely one of the strangest to
be displayed on the coat of arms of any clan.

Known as the green enfield, it features a weird hybrid
creature that has the tail of a lion, the body and hind legs of
a hound, the forelegs of an eagle, the mane of a horse, the
chest of an elephant, and the head of a fox.

The legend behind this curious creature goes back to one
of the greatest of the early Kellys, Tadhg Mór O'Kelly, and
to one of Ireland's most famous battles.

This was the battle of Clontarf, fought about four miles
north of Dublin on Good Friday of 1014.

Late tenth and early eleventh century Ireland was the
scene of vicious inter-clan rivalry as successive clan chiefs
fought for supremacy over their rivals.

It was this disunity that worked to the advantage of the
Norman invaders of the late twelfth century and the Viking
invaders of previous centuries.

The period 795 A.D. to 1014 A.D. is known to Irish

history as The Viking Tyranny, and it was largely through the inspired leadership of the great Irish hero king Brian Boru that Viking power was diminished, although not completely eliminated.

Boru was able to achieve this by managing to rally a number of other chieftains to his cause – although by no means all.

Among those who did rally to his banner was Tadhg Mór O'Kelly and his kinsfolk.

Boru, also known as Brian Bóruma and the ancestor of the distinguished O'Brien clan, was a son of Cennetig, king of Dál Cais, in the northern reaches of the province of Munster.

With his battle-hardened warriors known as the Dalcassian knights at his side, Boru had by 1002 A.D. achieved the prize of the High Kingship of Ireland – but there were still rival chieftains, and not least the Vikings, to deal with.

These Vikings, known as Ostmen, had occupied and fortified Dublin in the mid-ninth century and had other important trading settlements on other parts of the island.

Resenting Brian Boru's High Kingship, a number of chieftains, particularly those of the province of Leinster, found common cause with the Ostmen, and the two sides met in final and bloody confrontation at Clontarf.

Boru proved victorious, but the annals speak of great

slaughter on the day, with the dead piled high on the field of battle.

Among the many dead were not only Brian Boru's three sons, but also his faithful ally Tadhg Mór O'Kelly, who is reputed to have fallen 'fighting like a wolf dog.'

According to legend a strange animal surfaced from the depths of the nearby sea and protected O'Kelly's bloodied corpse until his clansmen could retrieve it for proper burial.

It is in memory of this curious incident that the animal known as the green enfield now appears not only on the Kelly crest, but can also be found incised on ancient Kelly tombstones.

Boru, meanwhile, had little time to celebrate his victory – being killed in his tent by a party of fleeing Vikings, but not before felling most of them with his great two-handed sword.

Kelly's were to be frequently found on the field of battle in subsequent centuries, notably in 1641 in the form of a rebellion by the Catholic landowners against the English Crown's policy of settling, or 'planting' loyal Protestants on Irish land.

This policy had started during the reign from 1491 to 1547 of Henry VIII, whose Reformation effectively outlawed the established Roman Catholic faith throughout his dominions.

In the insurrection that exploded in 1641, at least 2,000 Protestant settlers were massacred at the hands of Catholic landowners and their native Irish peasantry, while thousands more were stripped of their belongings and driven from their lands to seek refuge where they could.

Terrible as the atrocities were against the Protestant settlers, subsequent accounts became greatly exaggerated, serving to fuel a burning desire on the part of Protestants for revenge against the rebels.

Tragically for Ireland, this revenge became directed not only against the rebels, but native Irish such as the Kellys in general.

The English Civil War intervened to prevent immediate action against the rebels, but following the execution of Charles I in 1649 and the consolidation of the power of England's Oliver Cromwell, the time was ripe for revenge.

The Lord Protector, as he was named, descended on Ireland at the head of a 20,000-strong army that landed at Ringford, near Dublin, in August of 1649, and the consequences of this Cromwellian conquest still resonate throughout the island today.

Cromwell had three main aims: to quash all forms of rebellion, to 'remove' all Catholic landowners who had taken part in the rebellion, and to convert the native Irish to the Protestant faith.

An early warning of the terrors that were in store for the native Irish came when the northeastern town of Drogheda was stormed and taken in September and between 2,000 and 4,000 of its inhabitants killed.

The O'Kellys of Sligo were among those who suffered when their town was burned on the orders of the Cromwellian commander Sir Frederick Hamilton.

It was not long before Cromwell held Ireland in a grip of iron, allowing him to implement what amounted to a policy of ethnic cleansing.

His troopers were given free rein to hunt down and kill priests, while all Catholic estates were confiscated – leaving many Kellys dispossessed of the lands they had held for centuries.

Many joined the ranks of what are known as the Wild Geese – hunted men who became swords for hire to any foreign power that was an enemy of England.

The island exploded in a fury of discontent in the Rising of 1798, an ultimately abortive attempt to restore Irish freedom and independence.

The roots of the Rising are complex, but in essence it was sparked off by a fusion of sectarian and agrarian unrest and a desire for political reform that had been shaped by the French revolutionary slogan of 'liberty, equality, and fraternity.'

A movement had come into existence that embraced middle-class intellectuals and the oppressed peasantry, and if this loosely bound movement could be said to have had a leader, it was Wolfe Tone, a Protestant from Kildare and leading light of a radical republican movement known as the United Irishmen.

Despite attempts by the British government to concede a degree of agrarian and political reform, it was a case of far too little and much too late, and by 1795 the United Irishmen, through Wolfe Tone, were receiving help from France – Britain's enemy.

A French invasion fleet was despatched to Ireland in December of 1796, but it was scattered by storms off Bantry Bay.

Two years later, in the summer of 1798, rebellion broke out on the island, centred mainly in Co. Wexford.

The rebels achieved victory over the forces of the British Crown and militia known as yeomanry at the battle of Oulart Hill, followed by another victory at the battle of Three Rocks, but the peasant army was no match for the 20,000 troops or so that descended on Wexford.

Defeat followed at the battle of Vinegar Hill on 21 June, followed by another decisive defeat at Kilcumney Hill five days later.

One of the heroes of the rebellion was 25-year-old John Kelly, the son of a farmer from Killan, and who is commemorated today in the rousing ballad *Kelly from Killan*.

Captured after being wounded, he was hanged and decapitated in Wexford town and his head later kicked along the street by the triumphant and drunken yeomanry.

Chapter four:

On the world stage

Generations of Kellys, in all the variety of spellings of the name, have achieved fame and distinction, plus a fair degree of notoriety, both in the Emerald Isle itself and in those lands where their forefathers settled.

Eugene Curran Kelly, born in Pittsburgh, Pennsylvania, in 1912, was the actor, singer, dancer, choreographer, director, and producer best known as star of the silver screen **Gene Kelly**.

Named by the American Film Institute as among the greatest male stars of all time Kelly, who died in 1966, is famous for his performance in the 1952 movie *Singin' in The Rain*, although his first film role was beside Judy Garland in the 1942 *For Me and My Gal*.

He also starred with Garland in the 1951 *An American in Paris*.

Born in Vancouver, British Columbia, in 1924, **Barbara Kelly**, along with her husband Bernard Braden, became popular figures on British television after the couple moved to the United Kingdom in 1949. Kelly, who died in January of 2007, is probably best remembered as a panellist on the *What's My Line* television show.

It was as Dr Leonard 'Bones' McCoy, the doctor in the hugely popular *Star Trek* television series that actor

Jackson DeForest Kelley, born in Atlanta, Georgia, in 1920, will be best remembered. Kelly, who died in 1999, also starred in a number of *Star Trek* movies.

A real life space explorer, meanwhile, is **Scott Kelly**, the U.S. astronaut and naval aviator born in Orange, New Jersey, in 1964. A member of the Association of Space explorers and the Society of Experimental Test Pilots, at the time of writing he has logged nearly 200 hours in space.

Don O'Kelley, born at Sheepshead Bay, New York, in 1924, was a leading American television actor of the 1950s and 1960s, while **Josh Kelley**, born in Augusta, Georgia, in 1980, is a talented singer and songwriter whose genres embrace both pop rock and blues rock.

Gerard Kelly, born in 1959, and who died in 2010, was the Scottish actor who appeared in a number of popular sitcoms, including *Scotch and Wry*, *City Limits*, and *Rab C. Nesbitt*, while **Henry Kelly** is an Irish television presenter and radio disc jockey.

One of the icons of the silver screen was **Grace Kelly**, born in Philadelphia in 1929 and whose father's family hailed from Newport, in Ireland's Co. Mayo.

She was famous not only as an Oscar winning actress for her role in the 1955 movie *The Country Girl*, but for her marriage a year later to Prince Rainer of Monaco, which gave her the title of Her Serene Highness the Princess of Monaco. She died in 1982.

In the world of sport, both her father, **John B. Kelly Snr.** and her brother, **John B. Kelly Jnr.** were prize-winning oarsmen.

Her father won a gold medal for single scull and one for double scull at the 1922 Paris Olympics. His son, who was also known as Kelly Kelly, was an Olympic bronze medal winner – and it was this medal that he gave to his sister as a wedding present on her marriage to Prince Rainer.

Her uncle, meanwhile, **George Kelly**, was a Pulitzer-prize winning playwright.

Michael Kelly, better known as **King Kelly**, born in Troy, New York, in 1857, was a colourful star of American Major League Baseball, and the subject of a popular song from 1893, *Slide, Kelly, Slide*.

A flamboyant character who made no secret of his love of a tipple or two, he was often accompanied in public by his valet and a pet monkey.

Kieran Kelly, born in 1978, was the Irish jump jockey who died as a result of a tragic racing accident at the age of only 25, while **Paul Kelly**, born in 1969 at Wagga Wagga, New South Wales, is a top Australian Rules footballer, who at the time of writing is captain of the Sydney Swans.

On the rugby pitch, **Malcolm O'Kelly**, born in 1974, is an Irish rugby player who at the time of writing plays at club level for Leinster and as a lock for Ireland's international team, while **Sean Kelly**, born in 1956 and from Curraghduff, in Co. Waterford, is a former professional bicycle racer whose victories include seven successive wins in the Paris-Nice stage race, a Grand Tour win, and nine Monument wins.

In the world of books, **Seamus O'Kelly**, born in 1881, was a noted Irish writer, while in contemporary times **Kitty Kelley**, born in Spokane, Washington, in 1942, is an investigative journalist and author whose controversial books include *Jackie Oh!* an unauthorised biography of Jacqueline Kennedy Onassis, and unauthorised biographies of Elizabeth Taylor, Frank Sinatra, Nancy Reagan, and the American Bush dynasty.

At the time of writing, a biography of Ophrah Winfrey is said to be planned.

Walter Kelly, who was born in Philadelphia, Pennsylvania, in 1913, was better known as the gifted cartoonist **Walt Kelly** who, in addition to contributing to such Walt Disney classics as *Fantasia* and *Snow White and the Seven Dwarfs*, was the creator of the *Pogo* comic strip. He died in 1973.

On the field of battle, **Patrick Kelly**, originally from Castlehackett, in Co. Galway, became a leading commander of the Union army during the American Civil War, being promoted to the rank of Colonel.

As commander of the famed Irish Brigade, he saw action at the battle of Gettysburg in 1863, but was later killed in action at the siege of Petersburg while leading the brigade against Confederate defences.

During the First World War, **Christopher O'Kelly**, born in Winnipeg, Manitoba, in 1895, won a Victoria Cross – the highest award for gallantry for British and Commonwealth forces – for his behaviour in action at Passchendaele, Belgium, in October 1917.

As a captain in the 52nd (96th Lake Superior Regiment) battalion of the Canadian Expeditionary Force, he had led a company on a daring assault on German defences.

He was later promoted to the rank of major and survived the carnage of the war only to die in a boating accident in 1922 after serving for a time as prosecutor in North-western Ontario.

Two infamous Kellys include the Australian outlaw and folk hero **Ned Kelly** and the American gangster George Kelly, better known as **Machine Gun Kelly**.

Born near Melbourne in 1855, Ned Kelly was the son of John 'Red' Kelly, who had been transported to Tasmania in 1842 from his native Ireland after being sentenced to seven years penal servitude.

Ned and his gang of bushwhackers became infamous for a spree of bank robberies and murder that lasted nearly two years and ended in a final confrontation with the exasperated authorities at Glenrowan, in Victoria, in 1880.

Despite the protection of his homemade plate armour and helmet, Kelly was captured, tried, and sentenced to be hanged. The sentence was duly carried out in Melbourne Gaol, despite a petition signed by more than 30,000 ordinary citizens demanding that his life be spared.

Machine Gun Kelly, born in Memphis, Tennessee, in 1895, abandoned his studies at Mississippi State University in favour of a life of crime – his trademark weapon being the Thompson submachine gun.

He was eventually caught by the F.B.I in 1933 after a foiled kidnap attempt. Sentenced to life imprisonment, he died in Leavenworth Prison in 1954.

In he world of politics, **Sean T. O'Kelly**, born in Dublin in 1882, was an important figure in early twentieth century Irish politics, serving as 2nd President of the Irish Free State from 1945 until 1959, while **Sharon Kelly**, born in Washington State in 1944, served from 1991 to 1995 as mayor of Washington – the first African-American female to serve in such a post in a major U.S. city.

In the world of business and invention, **William Kelly**, born Pittsburgh, Pennsylvania, in 1811, was an iron manufacturer who, along with Henry Bessemer, invented the technique for producing iron through injecting air into molten metal.

Welsh-born **Dr. David Kelly** was the former United nations weapons inspector, expert in biological warfare, and employee of Britain's Ministry of Defence, who became the centre of controversy after apparently disclosing information concerning the U.K. government's dossier on Iraq's alleged weapons of mass destruction to a journalist.

He was found dead near his home in Oxfordshire in July of 2003 – a short time after having appeared before a committee of the House of Commons.

A formal verdict of suicide was recorded, but there are some who claim that rather more sinister factors could have contributed to his death.

In the cerebral world of chess, the grandly named **Alberic O'Kelly de Galway**, born in Brussels in 1911, and who died in 1980, was an International Chess Grand master, while in the equally cerebral world of statistics, the **Kelly Criterion** is a formula in probability theory for maximally investing money that was devised in 1956 by **J.L. Kelly Jnr**.

Key dates in Ireland's history from the first settlers to the formation of the Irish Republic:

circa 7000 B.C.	Arrival and settlement of Stone Age people.
circa 3000 B.C.	Arrival of settlers of New Stone Age period.
circa 600 B.C.	First arrival of the Celts.
200 A.D.	Establishment of Hill of Tara, Co. Meath, as seat of the High Kings.
circa 432 A.D.	Christian mission of St. Patrick.
800-920 A.D.	Invasion and subsequent settlement of Vikings.
1002 A.D.	Brian Boru recognised as High King.
1014	Brian Boru killed at battle of Clontarf.
1169-1170	Cambro-Norman invasion of the island.
1171	Henry II claims Ireland for the English Crown.
1366	Statutes of Kilkenny ban marriage between native Irish and English.
1529-1536	England's Henry VIII embarks on religious Reformation.
1536	Earl of Kildare rebels against the Crown.
1541	Henry VIII declared King of Ireland.
1558	Accession to English throne of Elizabeth I.
1565	Battle of Affane.
1569-1573	First Desmond Rebellion.
1579-1583	Second Desmond Rebellion.
1594-1603	Nine Years War.
1606	Plantation' of Scottish and English settlers.
1607	Flight of the Earls.
1632-1636	Annals of the Four Masters compiled.
1641	Rebellion over policy of plantation and other grievances.
1649	Beginning of Cromwellian conquest.
1688	Flight into exile in France of Catholic Stuart monarch James II as Protestant Prince William of Orange invited to take throne of England along with his wife, Mary.
1689	William and Mary enthroned as joint monarchs; siege of Derry.
1690	Jacobite forces of James defeated by William at battle of the Boyne (July) and Dublin taken.

1691	Athlone taken by William; Jacobite defeats follow at Aughrim, Galway, and Limerick; conflict ends with Treaty of Limerick (October) and Irish officers allowed to leave for France.
1695	Penal laws introduced to restrict rights of Catholics; banishment of Catholic clergy.
1704	Laws introduced constricting rights of Catholics in landholding and public office.
1728	Franchise removed from Catholics.
1791	Foundation of United Irishmen republican movement.
1796	French invasion force lands in Bantry Bay.
1798	Defeat of Rising in Wexford and death of United Irishmen leaders Wolfe Tone and Lord Edward Fitzgerald.
1800	Act of Union between England and Ireland.
1803	Dublin Rising under Robert Emmet.
1829	Catholics allowed to sit in Parliament.
1845-1849	The Great Hunger: thousands starve to death as potato crop fails and thousands more emigrate.
1856	Phoenix Society founded.
1858	Irish Republican Brotherhood established.
1873	Foundation of Home Rule League.
1893	Foundation of Gaelic League.
1904	Foundation of Irish Reform Association.
1913	Dublin strikes and lockout.
1916	Easter Rising in Dublin and proclamation of an Irish Republic.
1917	Irish Parliament formed after Sinn Fein election victory.
1919-1921	War between Irish Republican Army and British Army.
1922	Irish Free State founded, while six northern counties remain part of United Kingdom as Northern Ireland, or Ulster; civil war up until 1923 between rival republican groups.
1949	Foundation of Irish Republic after all remaining constitutional links with Britain are severed.